The Novello Primary Chorals

easy **ABBA**

Published by
Novello Publishing Limited
14-15 Berners Street, London W1T 3LJ, UK.

Exclusive distributors:
Music Sales Limited
Distribution Centre, Newmarket Road, Bury St Edmunds, Suffolk, IP33 3YB.

Music Sales Pty Limited
20 Resolution Drive, Caringbah, NSW 2229, Australia.

Order No. NOV940720
ISBN 978-1-84938-063-8
This collection © Copyright 2009 Novello & Company Limited.

Printed in the EU.

www.musicsales.com

Novello Publishing L
part of The Music Sal

London / New York / Paris / Sydney / Copenhagen / Berlin / Madrid / Tokyo

Dancing Queen

Words & Music by Benny Andersson, Stig Anderson & Björn Ulvaeus

3

watch that scene, dig-gin' the danc-ing queen.

watch that scene, dig-gin' the danc-ing queen.

1. Fri - day night and the lights are low,_____

1. Fri - day night and the lights are low,_____

4

look-ing out__ for a place to go,__

look-ing out__ for a place to go,__

where they play__ the right mu - sic, get-ting in__ the swing. You come to

where they play__ the right mu - sic, get-ting in__ the swing. You come to

look for a king.__

look for a king.__

To Coda ⊕

I Have A Dream

Words & Music by Benny Andersson & Björn Ulvaeus

Easy ballad style

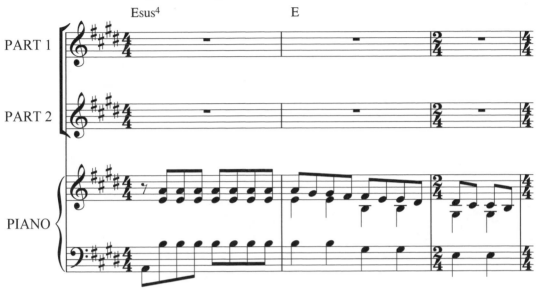

12

13

15

Mamma Mia

Words & Music by Benny Andersson, Stig Anderson & Björn Ulvaeus

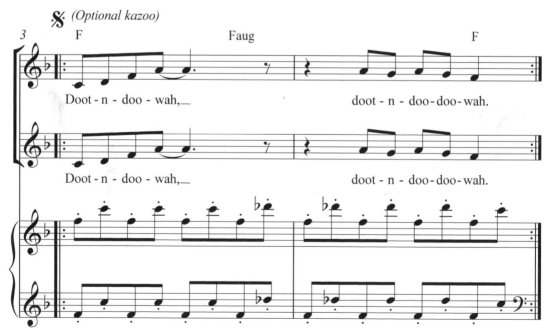

17

So I made up my mind,___ it is o - ver now.
I can't count all the times___ that I've said we're through.

Look at me now,___ will I ev - er learn?
And when you go,___ when you slam the door,

Look at me now,___ will I ev - er learn?
And when you go,___ when you slam the door,

I don't know how___ but I sud - den - ly lose_
I think you know_ that you won't be a - way_

I don't know how___ but I sud - den - ly lose_
I think you know_ that you won't be a - way_

21

Super Trouper

Words & Music by Benny Andersson & Björn Ulvaeus

Steady, but with bounce

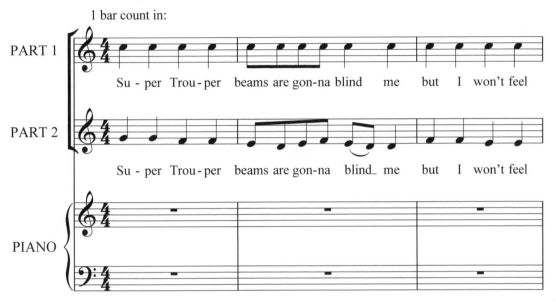

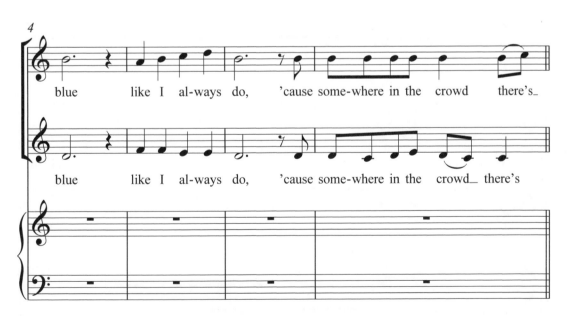

42

Csus⁴   C   G   Dm

but I won't feel blue   like I al - ways

but I won't feel blue   like I al - ways

45 G   *To Coda* ⊕

do,   'cause some-where in the crowd there's_

do,   'cause some-where in the crowd_ there's

47 C   F

you.   So I'll be there when you ar-

you.   So I'll be there when you ar-

28

29

Thank You For The Music

Words & Music by Benny Andersson & Björn Ulvaeus

giv-ing it to me.___

giv-ing it to me.___

I've been so luck-y.___

I am the child___

___ with gold-en hair. I wan-na sing___ it out to

I wan-na sing___ it out to

Waterloo

Words & Music by Benny Andersson, Stig Anderson & Björn Ulvaeus

Bright shuffle

1. My, my,—

1. My, my,—

37

41

The Winner Takes It All

Words & Music by Benny Andersson & Björn Ulvaeus

Heart-felt ballad

44

CD Track Listing

1. Dancing Queen
(Andersson/Anderson/Ulvaeus)
Bocu Music Limited

2. I Have A Dream
(Andersson/Ulvaeus)
Bocu Music Limited

3. Mamma Mia
(Andersson/Anderson/Ulvaeus)
Bocu Music Limited

4. Super Trouper
(Andersson/Ulvaeus)
Bocu Music Limited

5. Thank You For The Music
(Andersson/Ulvaeus)
Bocu Music Limited

6. Waterloo
(Andersson/Anderson/Ulvaeus)
Bocu Music Limited

7. The Winner Takes It All
(Andersson/Ulvaeus)
Bocu Music Limited